EASY PIANO

T0081516

CHRIS TOMLIN
ARRIVING

ISBN-13: 978-1-4234-2537-3
ISBN-10: 1-4234-2537-5

HAL•LEONARD®
CORPORATION
7777 W. BLUEMOUND RD. P.O. BOX 13819 MILWAUKEE, WI 53213

Visit Hal Leonard Online at
www.halleonard.com

www.christomlin.com

INDESCRIBABLE

Words and Music by LAURA STORY
and JESSE REEVES

Brightly, in one

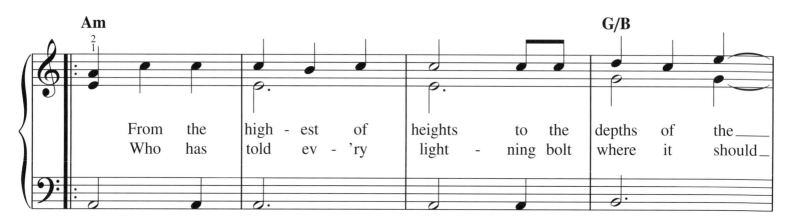

From the high - est of heights to the depths of the____
Who has told ev - 'ry light - ning bolt where it should__

__ sea,
__ go

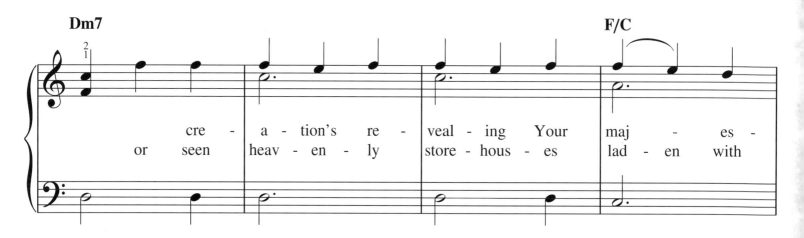

cre - a - tion's re - veal - ing Your maj - es -
or seen heav - en - ly store - hous - es lad - en with

Bb

ty.
snow?

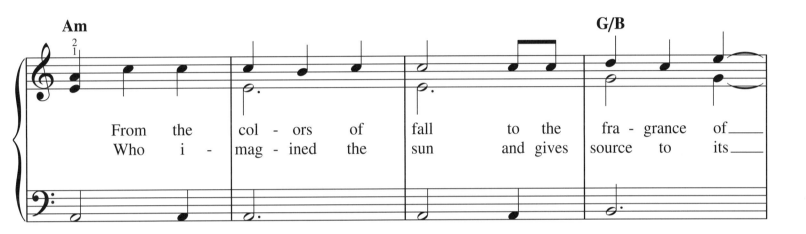

Am   **G/B**

From the col - ors of fall to the fra - grance of___
Who i - mag - ined the sun and gives source to its___

C

___ spring,
___ light,

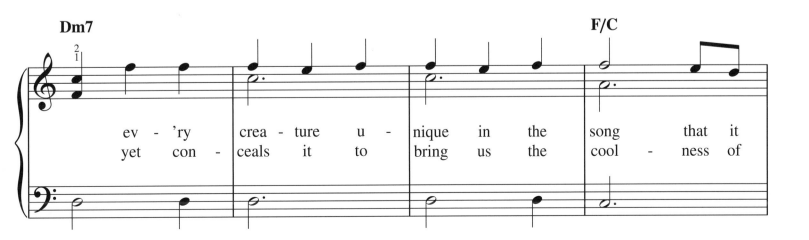

Dm7   **F/C**

ev - 'ry crea - ture u - nique in the song that it
yet con - ceals it to bring us the cool - ness of

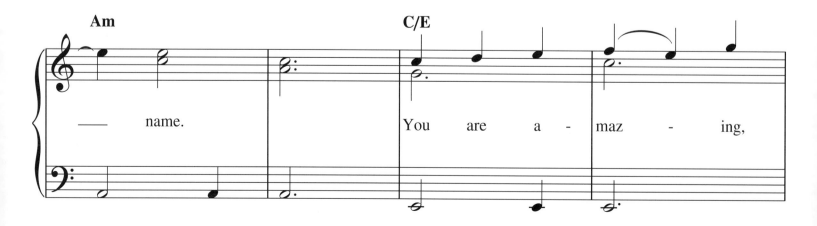

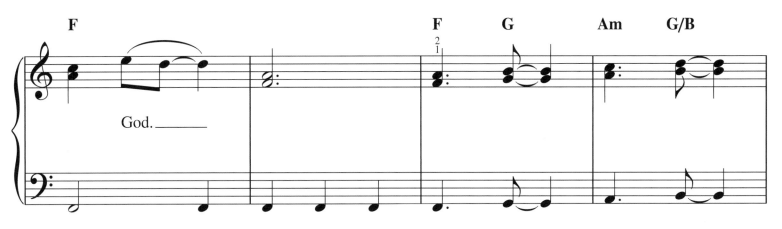

God._____

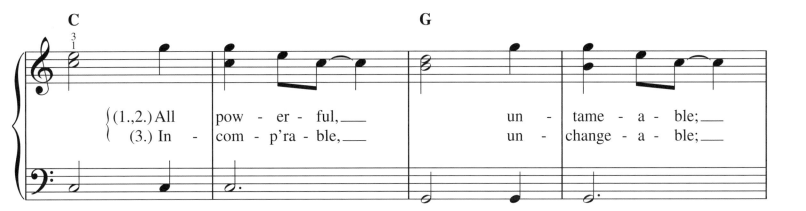

{(1.,2.) All | pow - er - ful,___ | un - | tame - a - ble;___
{ (3.) In - | com - p'ra - ble,___ | un - | change - a - ble;___

awe - struck, we | fall to our | knees as we | hum - bly pro -
You see the | depths of my | heart and You | love me the___

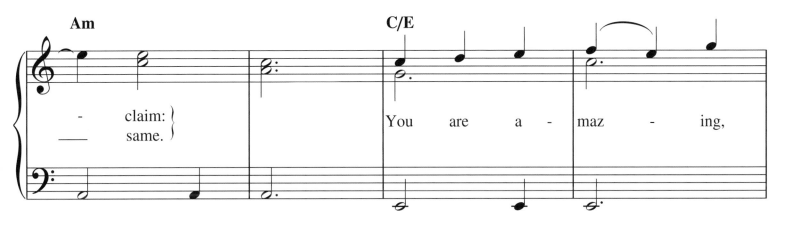

- claim: } | | You are a - maz - | ing,
___ same. }

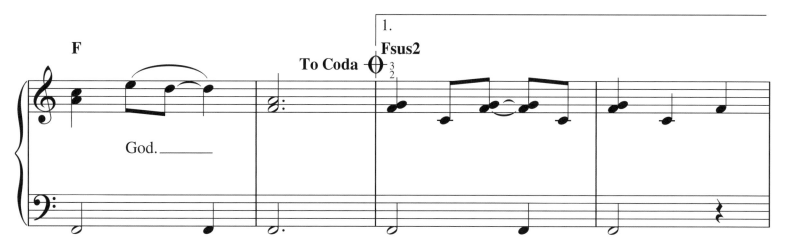

God._____

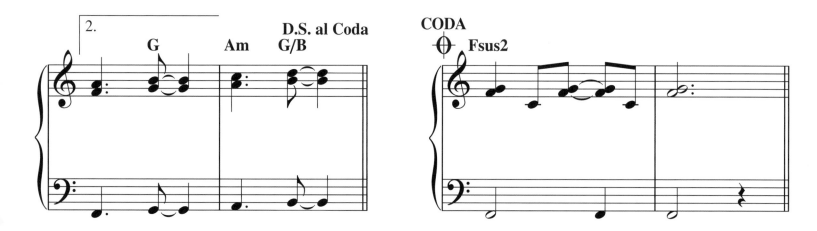

HOLY IS THE LORD

Words and Music by CHRIS TOMLIN
and LOUIE GIGLIO

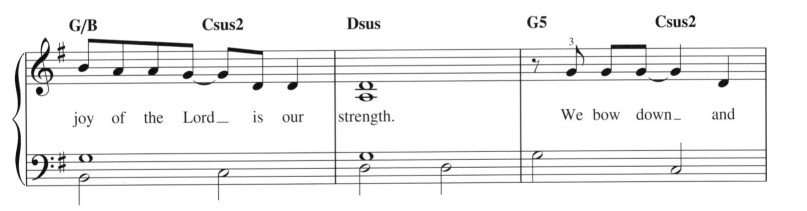

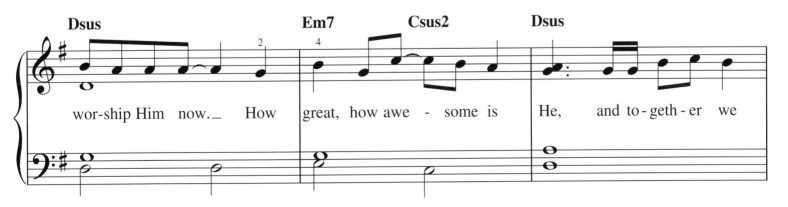

8

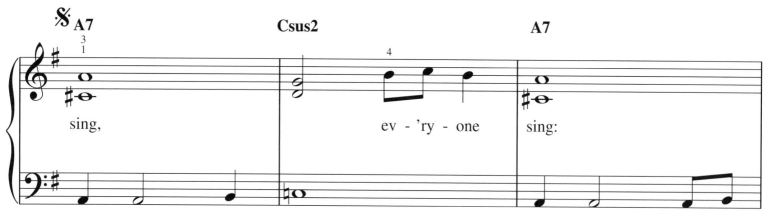

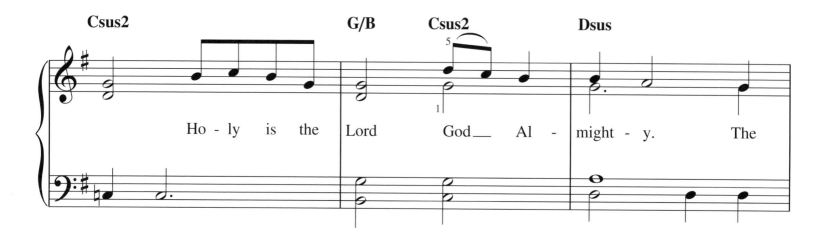

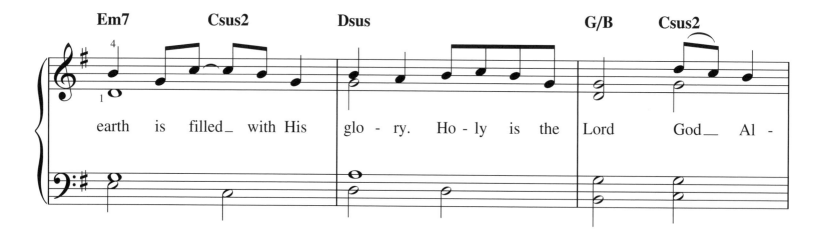

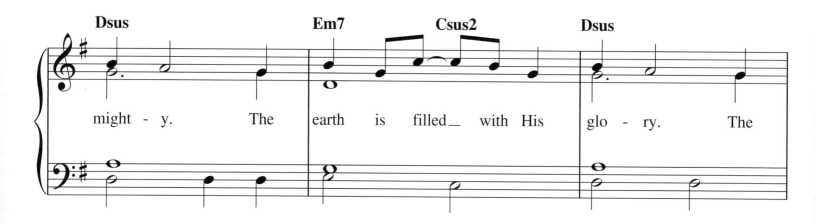

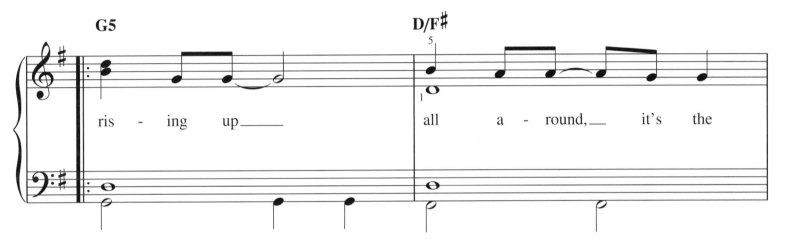

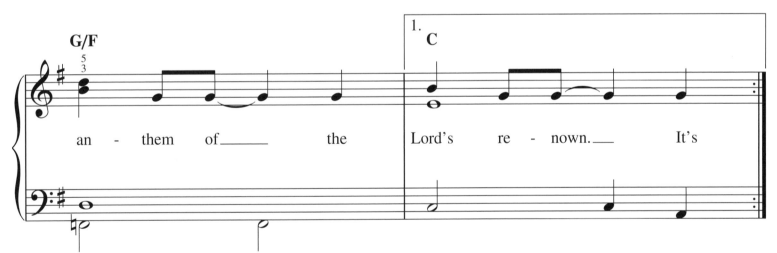

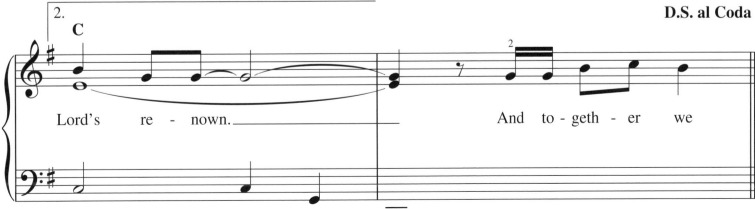

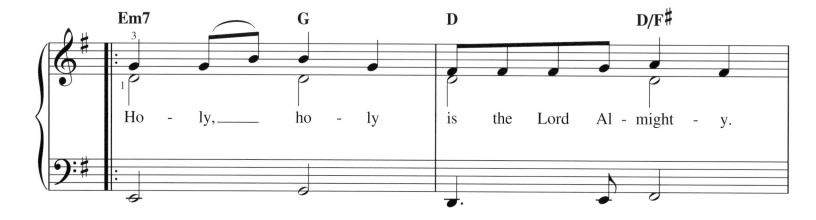

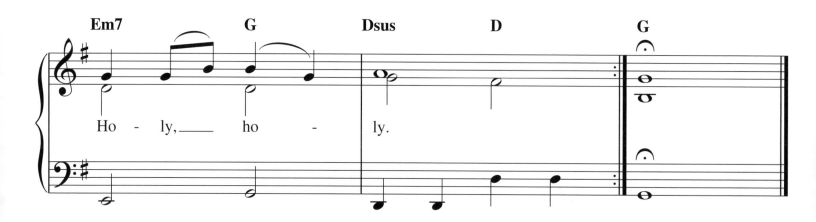

HOW GREAT IS OUR GOD

Words and Music by CHRIS TOMLIN,
JESSE REEVES and ED CASH

With praise

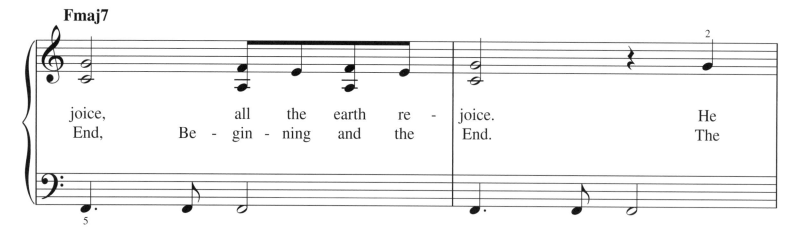

C

great   is   our   God!   Sing   with   me: How

Am7

great   is   our   God!   And   all   will   see   how

Fmaj7   **G**   **C**

great,   how   great   is   our   God!

1.   2.

And

Name   a - bove_____   all   names,_____

wor - thy   of_____   all   praise._____   My

heart   will   sing:___   How   great   is   our   God!

great   is   our   God!

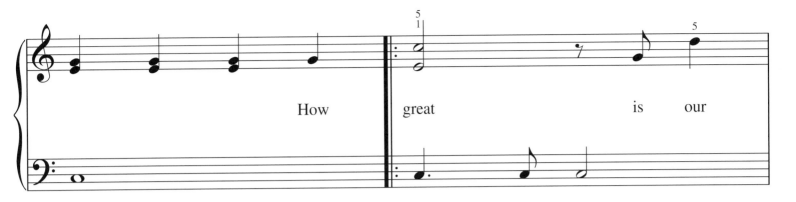

How great is our

God! Sing with me: How great is our

Am7

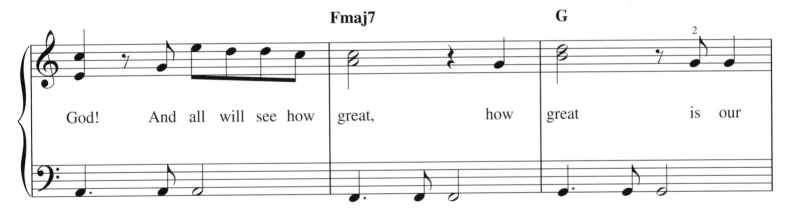

Fmaj7   **G**

God! And all will see how great, how great is our

1., 2.
C

God!   How

3.
C

God!

YOUR GRACE IS ENOUGH

Words and Music by
MATT MAHER

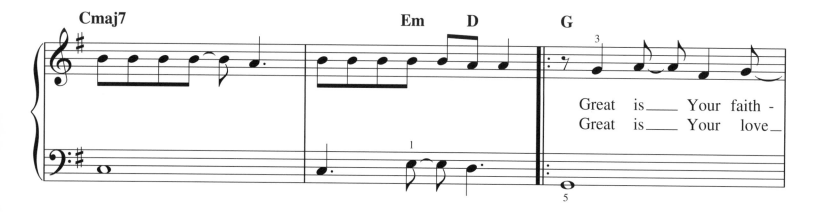

Great is___ Your faith -
Great is___ Your love_

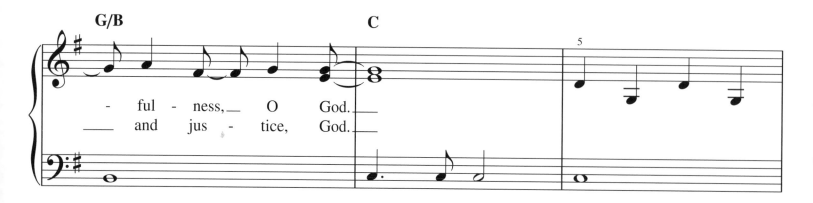

- ful - ness,_ O God._
__ and jus - tice, God._

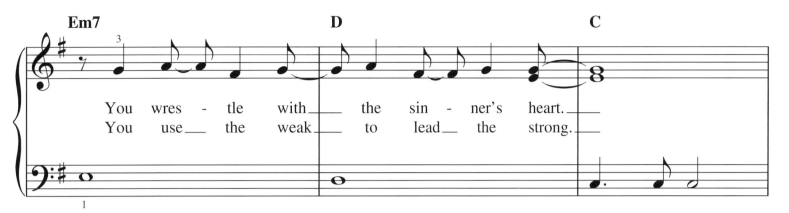

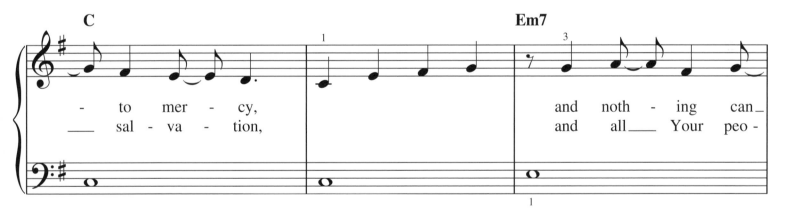

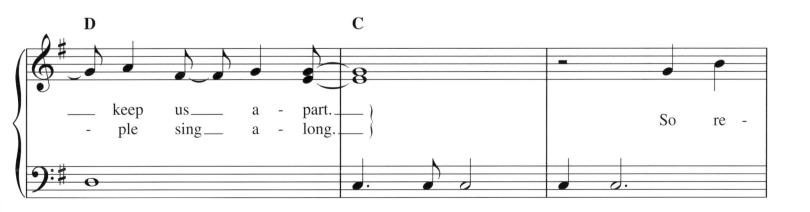

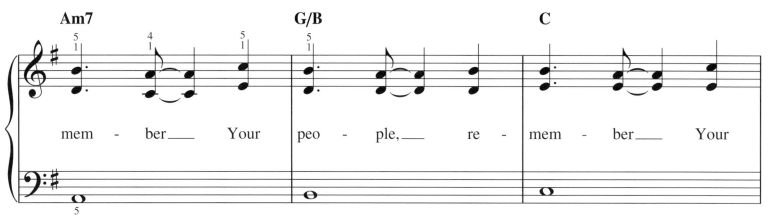

mem - ber___ Your peo - ple,___ re - mem - ber___ Your

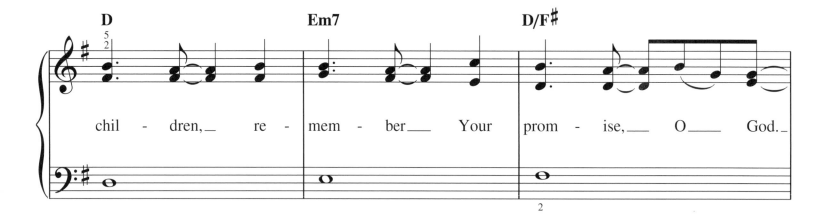

chil - dren,___ re - mem - ber___ Your prom - ise,___ O___ God.___

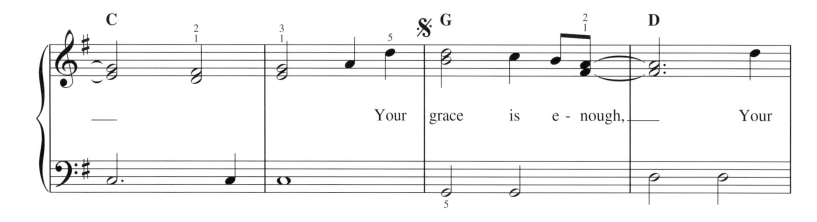

___ Your grace is e - nough,___ Your

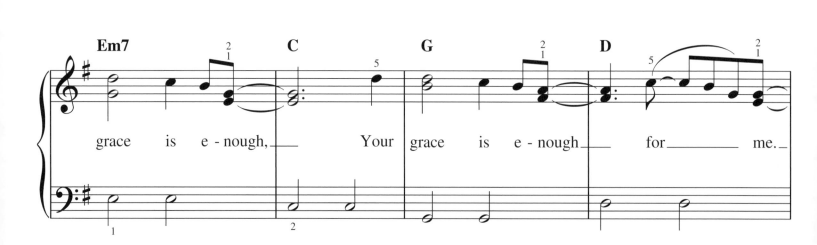

grace is e - nough,___ Your grace is e - nough___ for___ me.

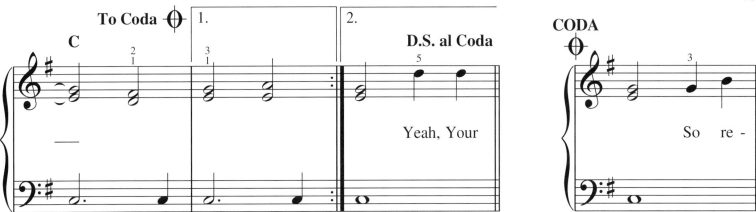

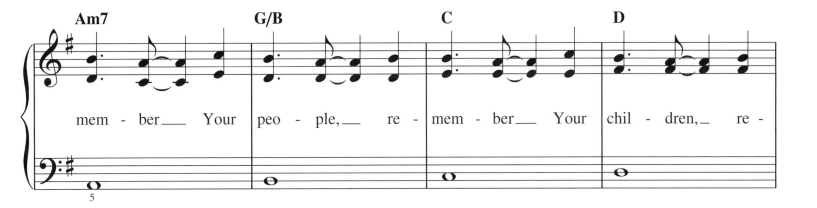

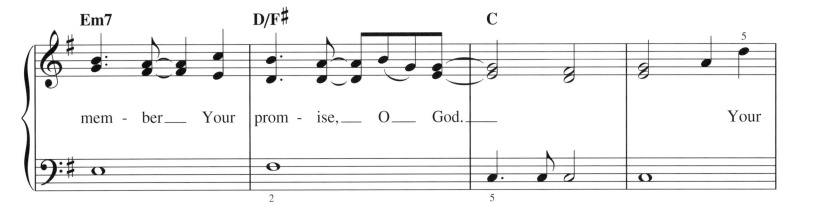

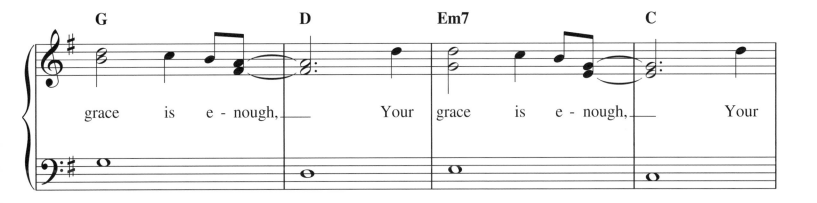

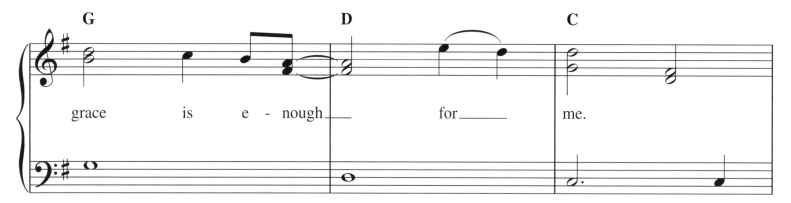

grace is e - nough____ for____ me.

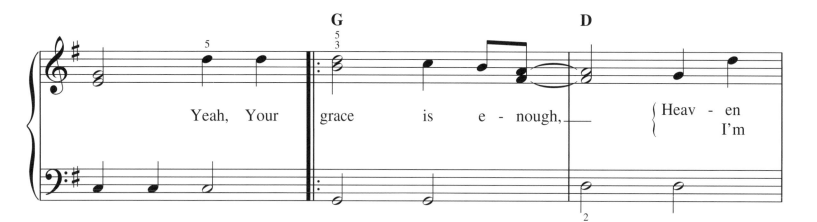

Yeah, Your grace is e - nough,____ { Heav - en / I'm

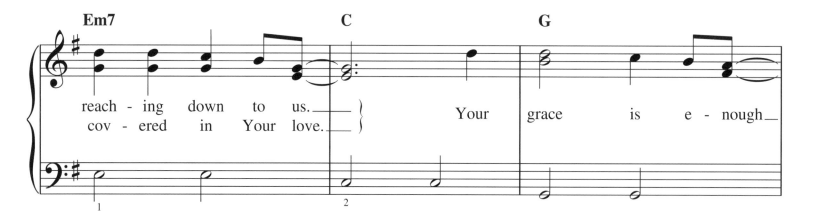

reach - ing down to us.____ }
cov - ered in Your love.____ } Your grace is e - nough__

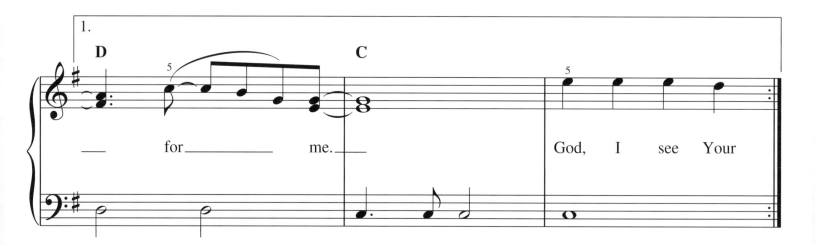

1.

_____ for_____ me._____ God, I see Your

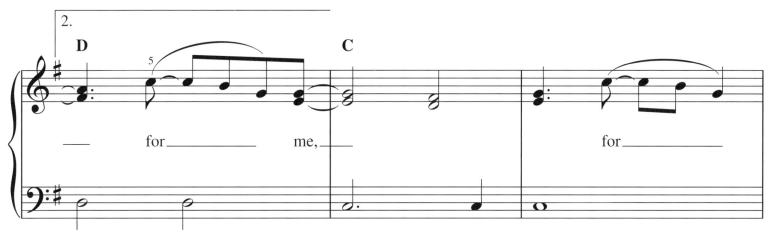

for _____ me, _____

for _____

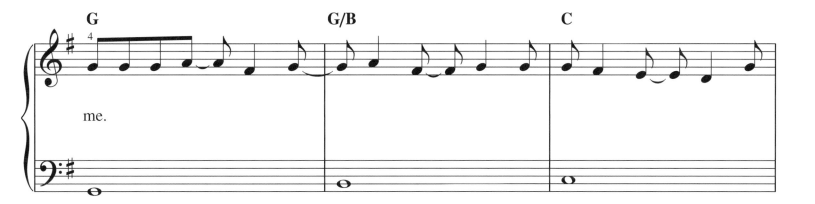

me.

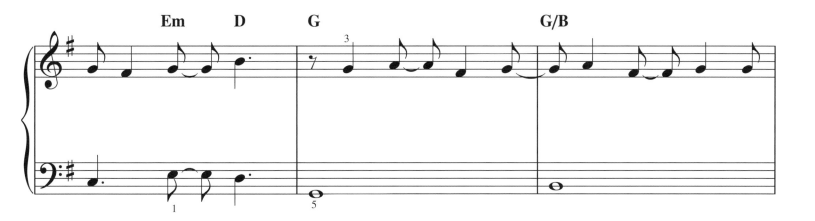

UNFAILING LOVE

Words and Music by CHRIS TOMLIN,
ED CASH and CARY PIERCE

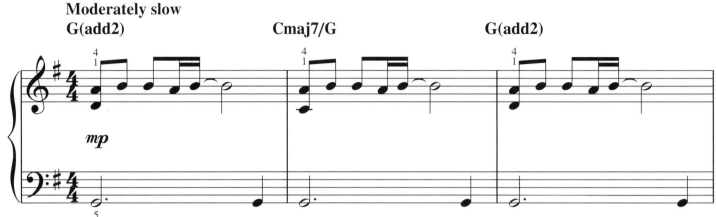

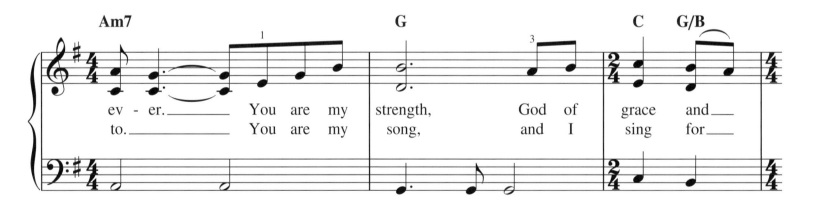

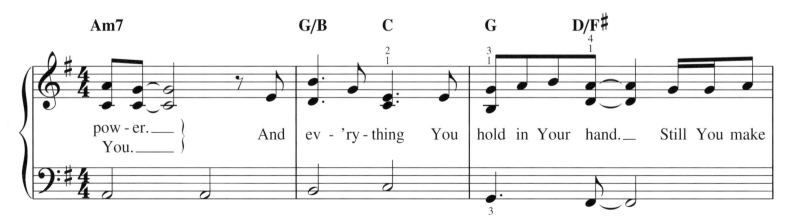

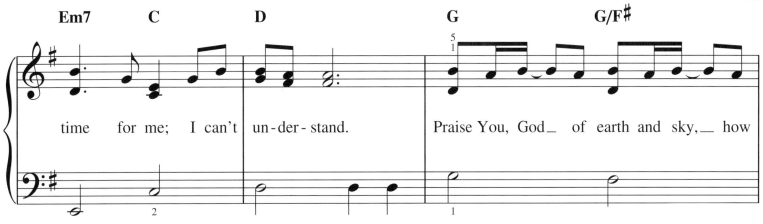

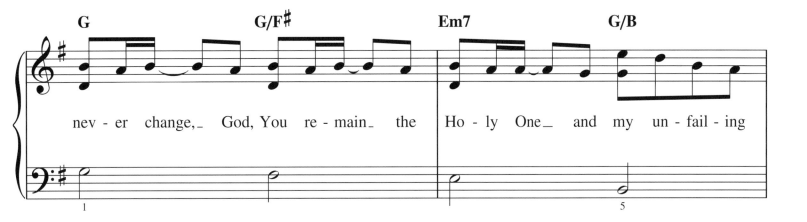

ev - 'ry - thing You hold in Your hand.__ Still You make time for me; I can't

un - der - stand. Praise You, God__ of earth and sky,__ how

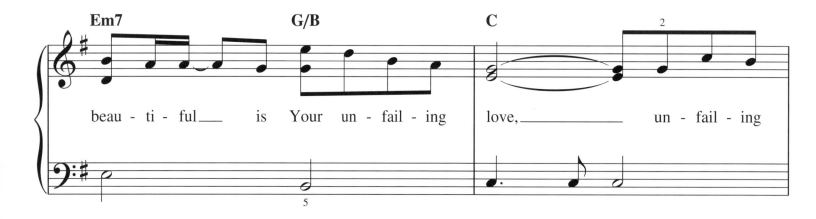

beau - ti - ful__ is Your un - fail - ing love,_____ un - fail - ing

love. And You nev - er change,__ God, You re - main__ the

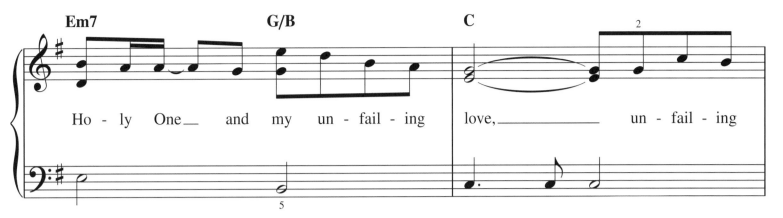

Em7   G/B   C

Ho - ly One___ and my un - fail - ing love, _____ un - fail - ing

1. Dsus

love.   I will praise You.

2. Dsus   C

love, _____ un - fail - ing love, _____ un - fail - ing

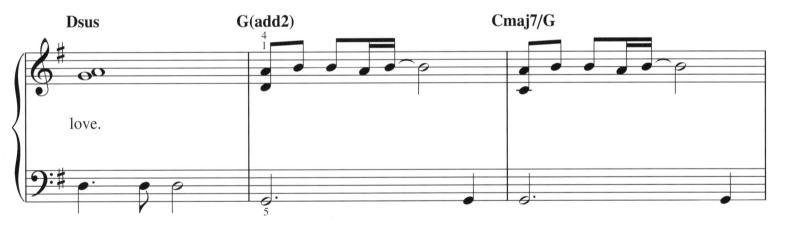

Dsus   G(add2)   Cmaj7/G

love.

G(add2)   Cmaj7/G   G

THE WAY I WAS MADE

Words and Music by CHRIS TOMLIN,
JESSE REEVES and ED CASH

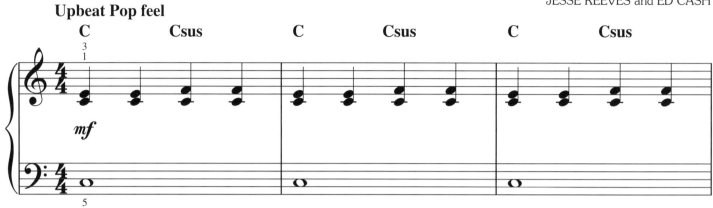

Caught in the half - light,

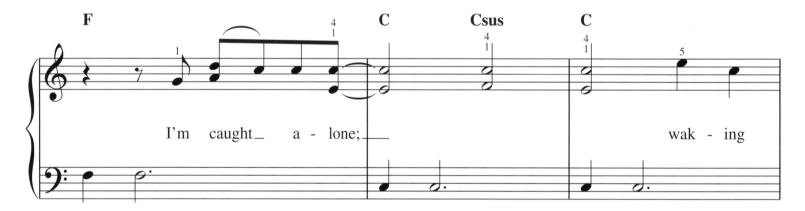

I'm caught_ a - lone;__ wak - ing

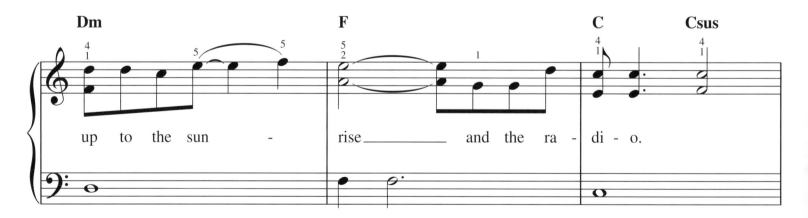

up to the sun - rise_____ and the ra - di - o.

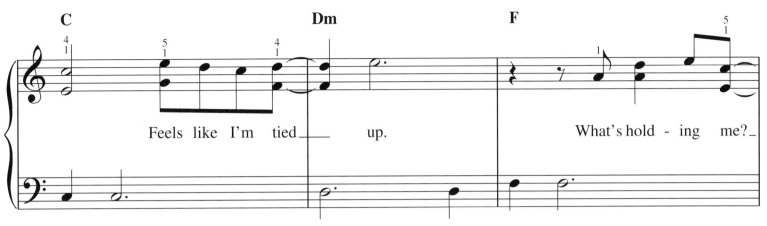

Feels like I'm tied___ up. What's hold - ing me?___

Just pray - ing to - day___ will be the day___

I go free.___ And I want to live like there's no to - mor -

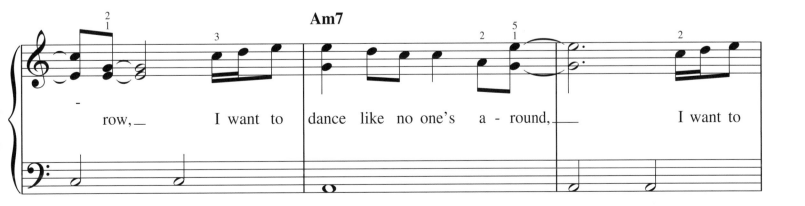

row,___ I want to dance like no one's a - round,___ I want to

sing like no-bod – y's lis – t'ning before I lay my bod-y down.

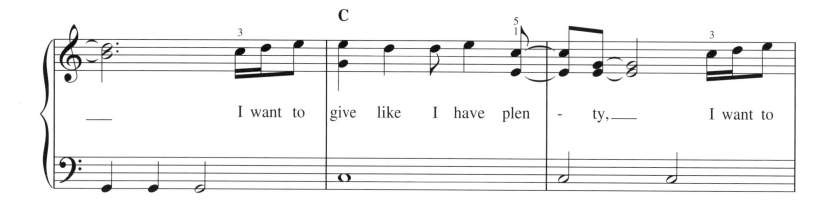

I want to give like I have plen – ty,___ I want to

love like I'm not a - fraid,___ I want to be the man___ I was meant___

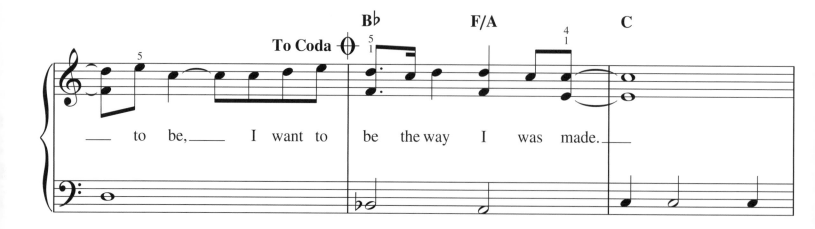

to be,___ I want to be the way I was made.___

Made in Your like - ness, made with Your hands.

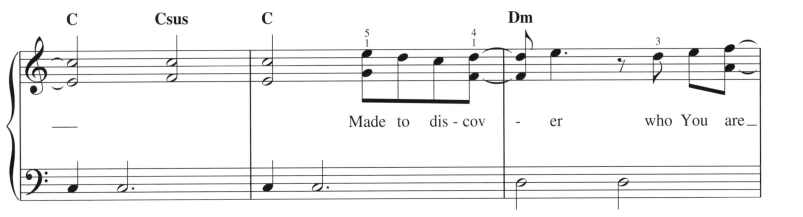

Made to dis - cov - er who You are

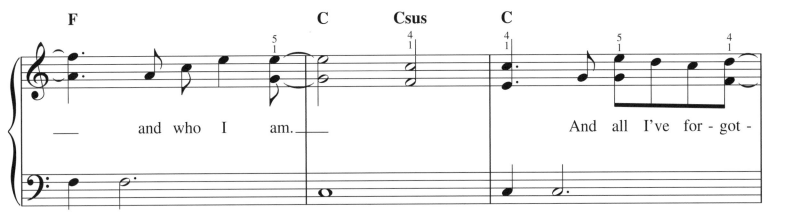

and who I am. And all I've for - got -

- ten, help me to find.

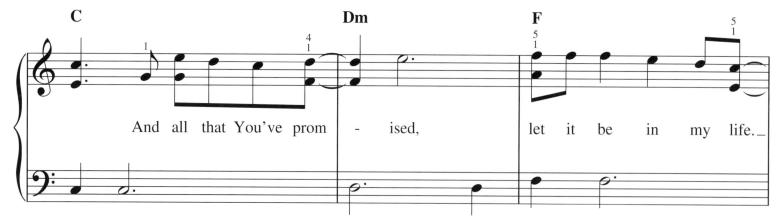

And all that You've prom - ised, let it be in my life.

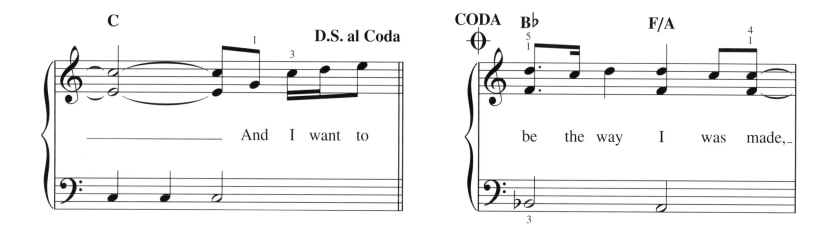

_____ And I want to

D.S. al Coda

CODA

be the way I was made,

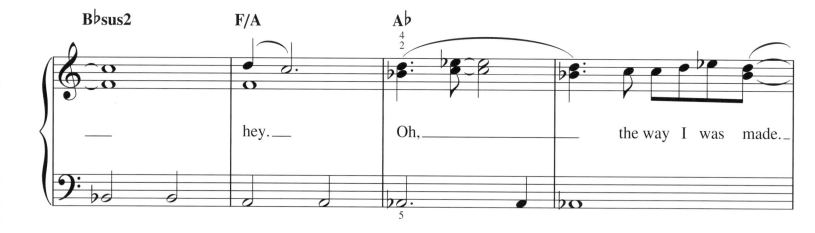

___ hey.___ Oh,_____ the way I was made.__

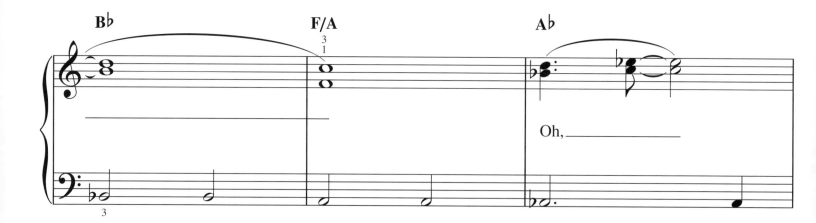

Oh,_____

oh._____ I want to live like there's no to - mor -

- row, I want to dance like no one's a - round,___ I want to

sing like no - bod - y's lis - t'ning be - fore I lay my bod - y down.__

I want to give like I have plen - ty,___ I want to

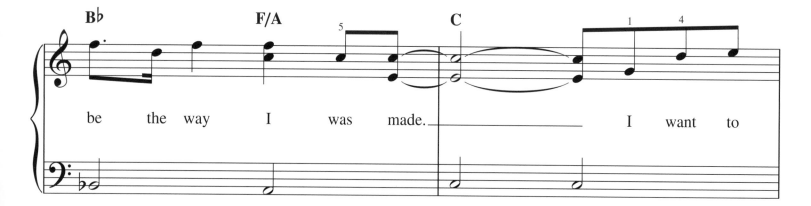

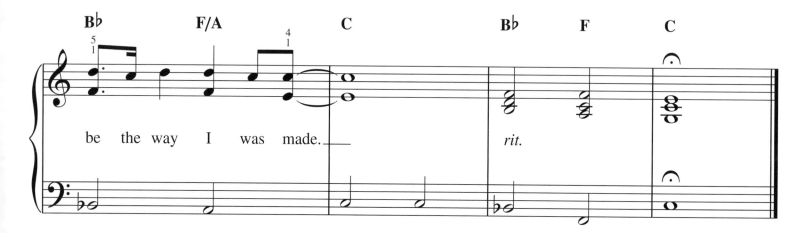

MIGHTY IS THE POWER OF THE CROSS

Words and Music by SHAWN CRAIG
and CHRIS TOMLIN

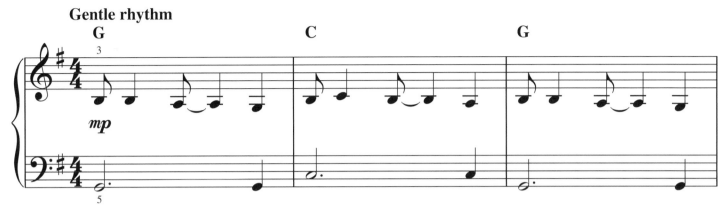

What can take a dy - ing man and
What re - stores our faith in God?

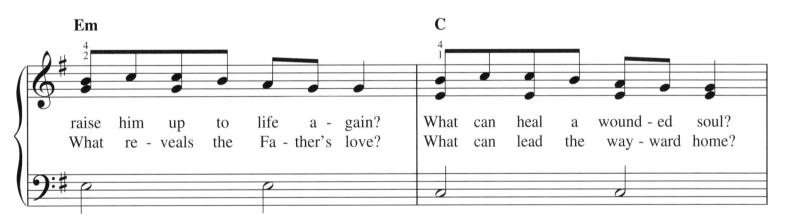

raise him up to life a - gain?   What can heal a wound - ed soul?
What re - veals the Fa - ther's love?   What can lead the way - ward home?

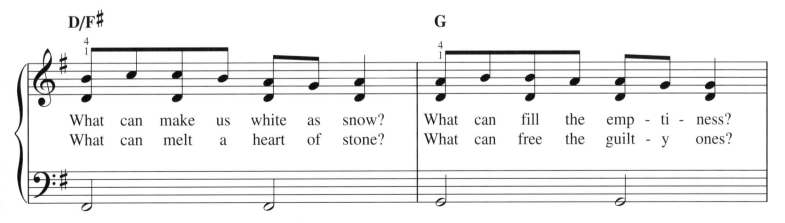

What can make us white as snow?   What can fill the emp - ti - ness?
What can melt a heart of stone?   What can free the guilt - y ones?

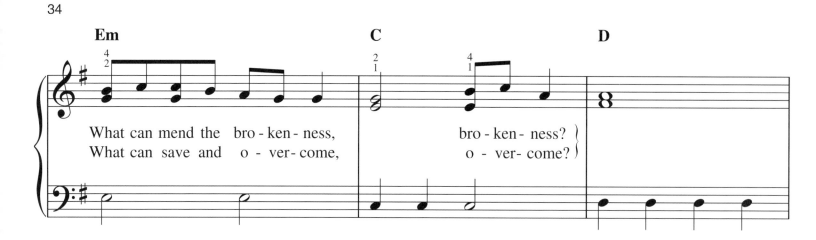

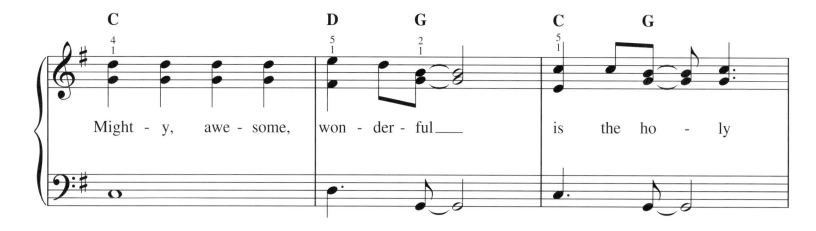

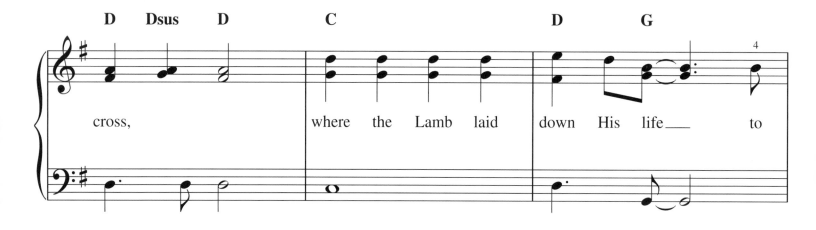

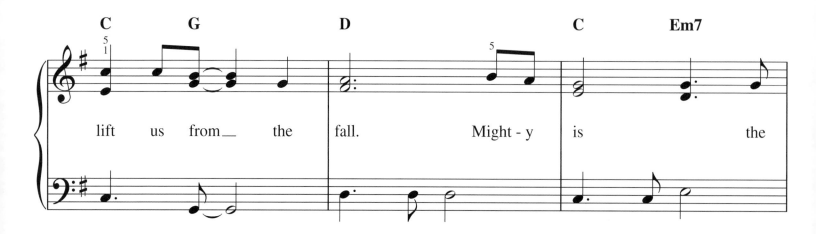

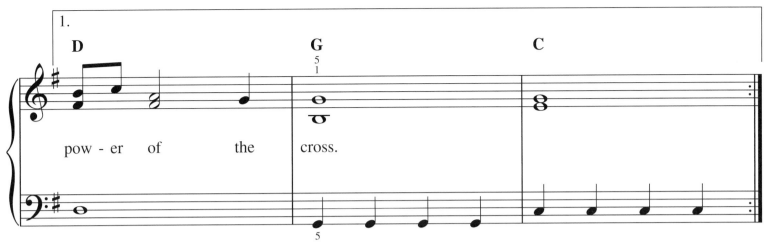

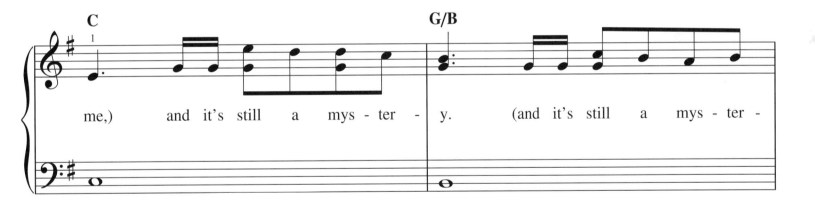

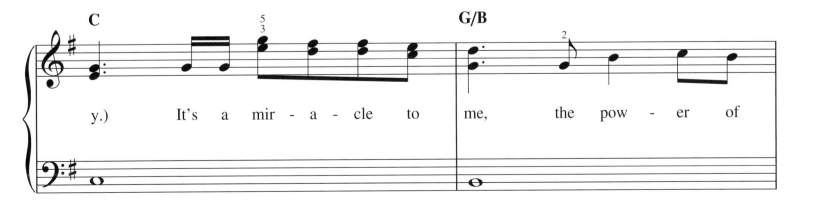

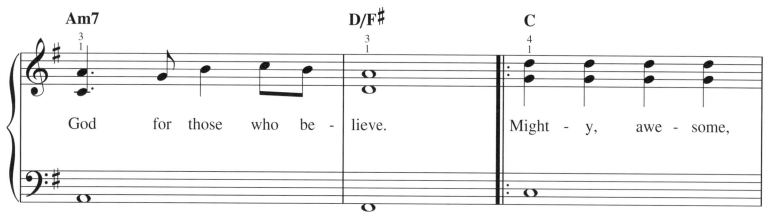

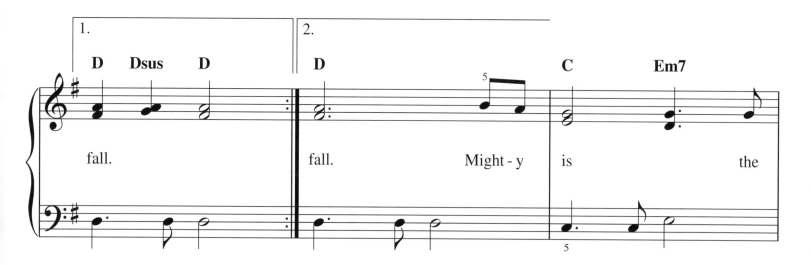

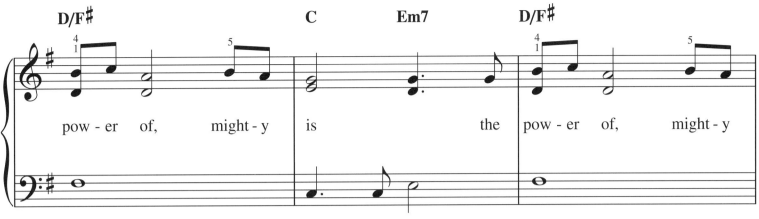

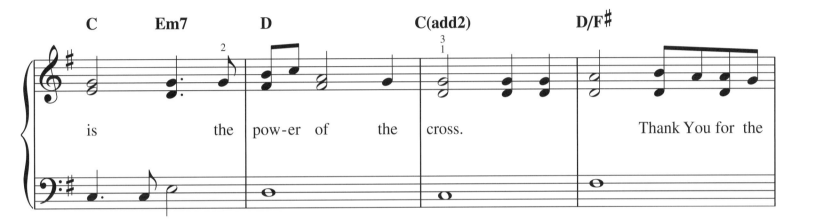

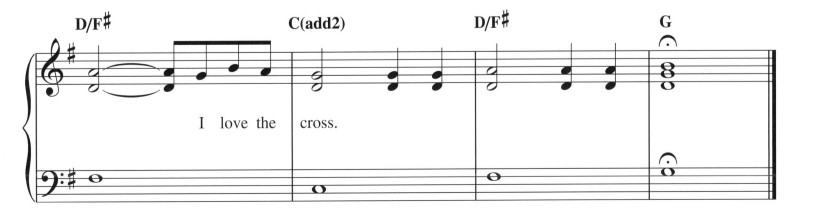

ALL BOW DOWN

Words and Music by CHRIS TOMLIN
and ED CASH

Moderate Rock feel

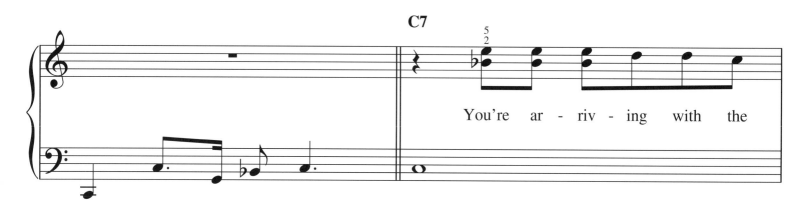

You're ar - riv - ing with the

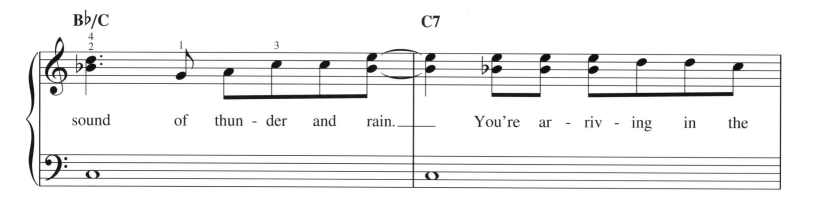

sound of thun - der and rain. You're ar - riv - ing in the

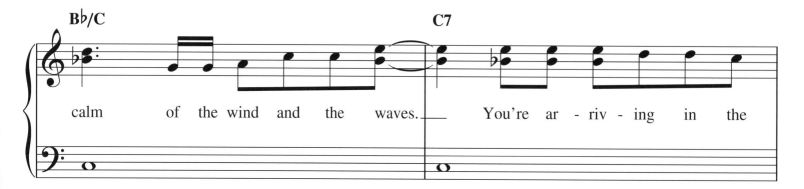

calm of the wind and the waves. You're ar - riv - ing in the

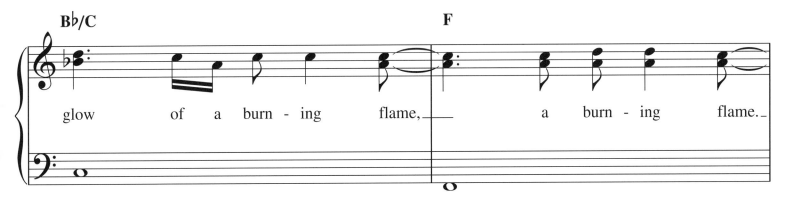

B♭/C   **F**

glow   of   a   burn - ing   flame,___   a   burn - ing   flame.___

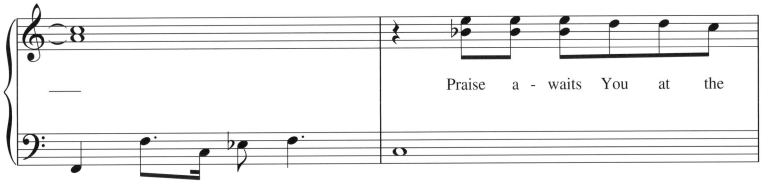

C7

___   Praise   a - waits   You   at   the

B♭/C   **C7**

dawn,   when the world comes a - live.___   Praise   a - waits   You   in   the

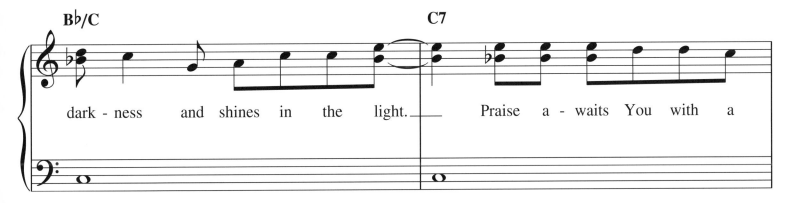

B♭/C   **C7**

dark - ness   and shines in the light.___   Praise   a - waits   You   with   a

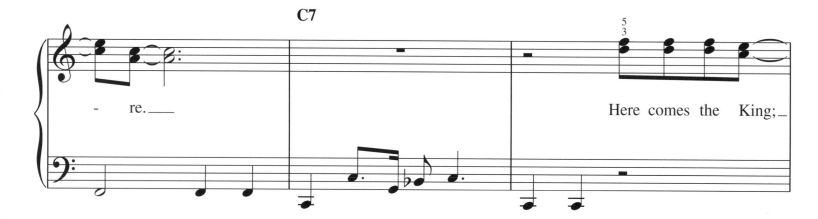

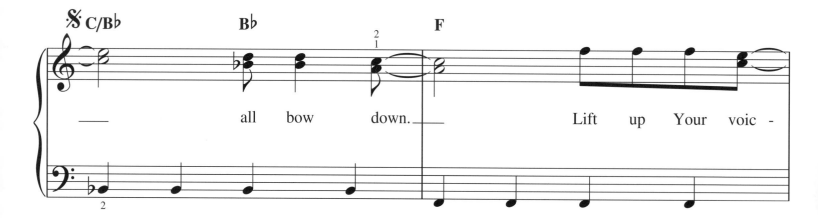

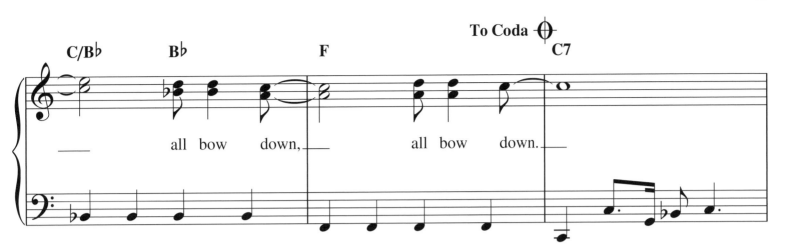

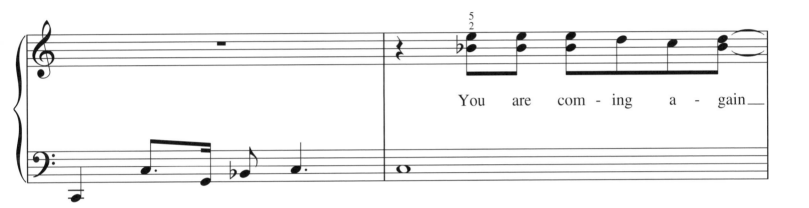

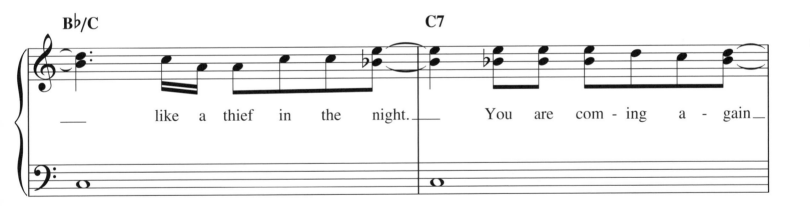

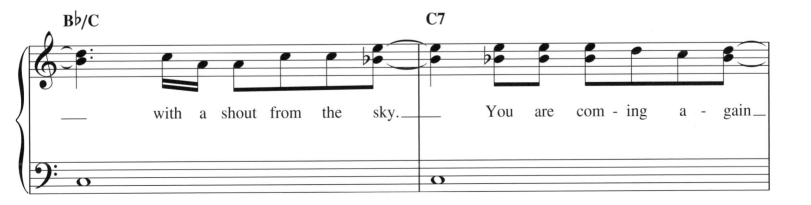

D.S. al Coda

to take a - way Your Bride, to take a - way Your Bride. Here comes the King;—

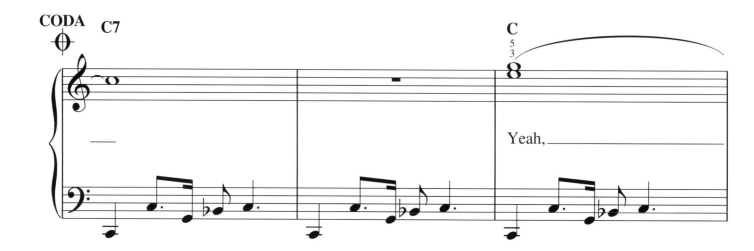

CODA

Yeah,————

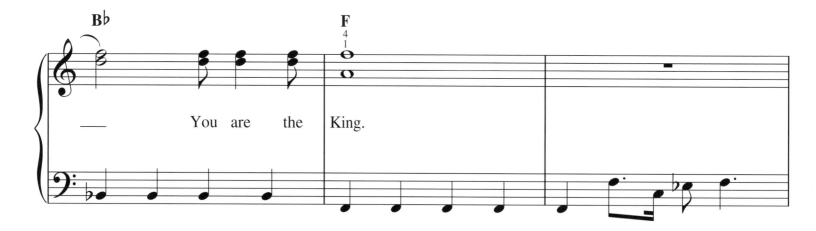

— You are the King.

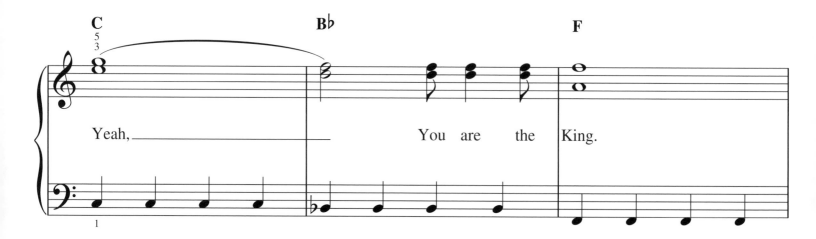

Yeah,———————— You are the King.

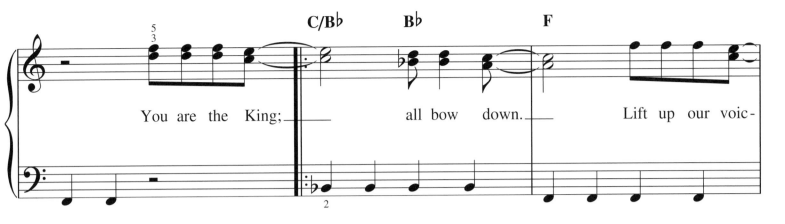

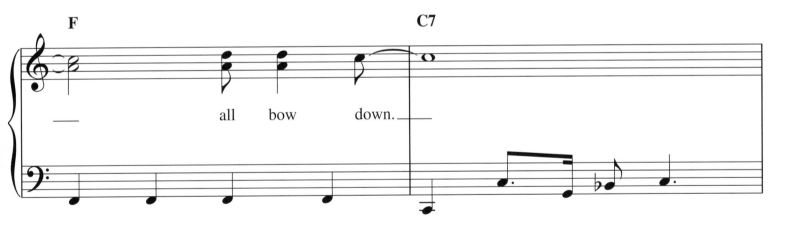

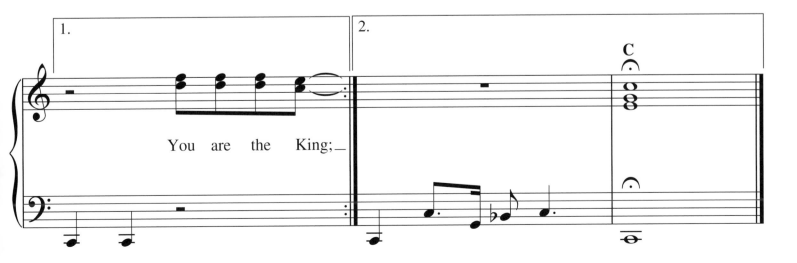

ON OUR SIDE

Words and Music by CHRIS TOMLIN,
JESSE REEVES and ED CASH

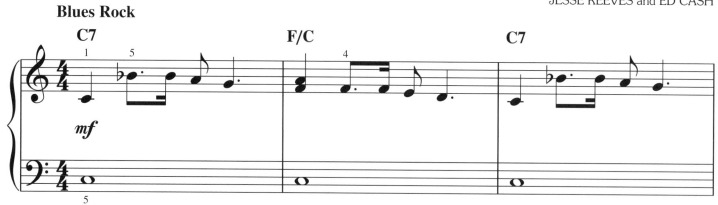

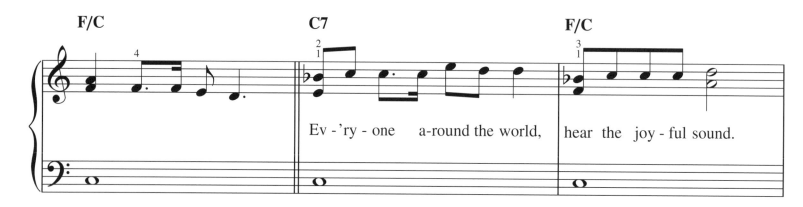

Ev-'ry-one a-round the world, hear the joy-ful sound.

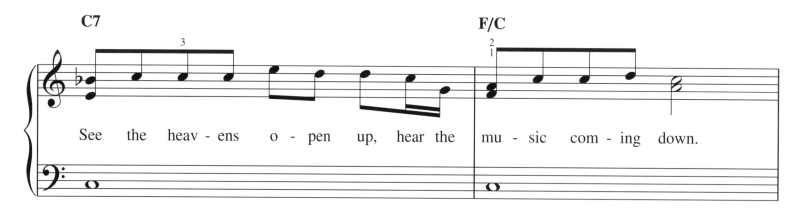

See the heav-ens o-pen up, hear the mu-sic com-ing down.

Noth-ing's gon-na sep-a-rate us from the Fa-ther's love. I can't help but cel-e-brate,

'cause we're not a-lone. If God is on___ our side, who can be a-gainst us? If God is

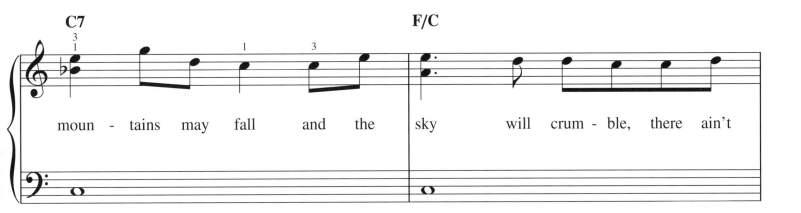

on___ our side, we won't be a - fraid.___ Though the

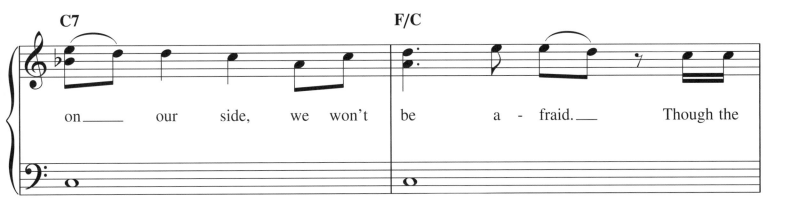

moun - tains may fall and the sky will crum - ble, there ain't

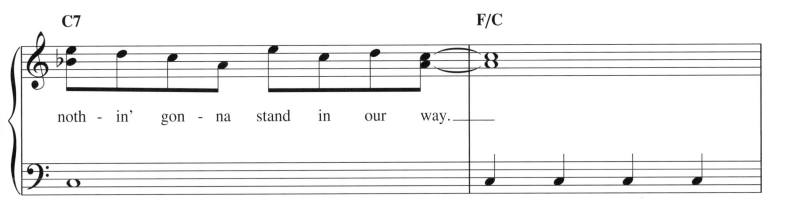

noth - in' gon - na stand in our way.___

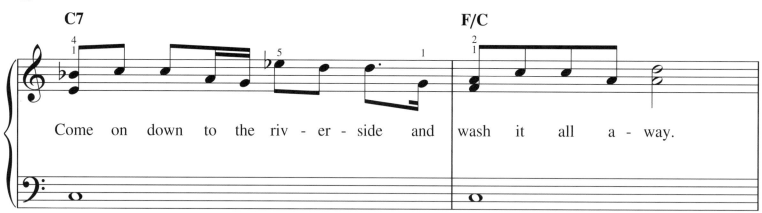

Come on down to the riv - er - side and wash it all a - way.

Leave be - hind your trou - bled mind for an un - cloud - y day.

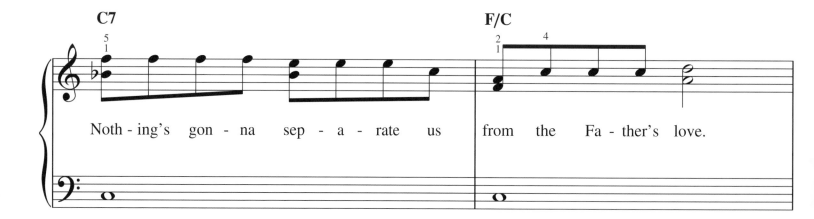

Noth - ing's gon - na sep - a - rate us from the Fa - ther's love.

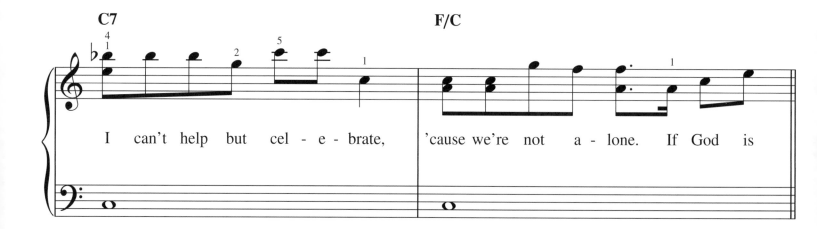

I can't help but cel - e - brate, 'cause we're not a - lone. If God is

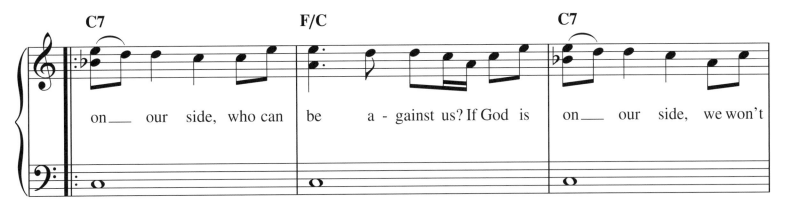

on___ our side, who can be a - gainst us? If God is on___ our side, we won't

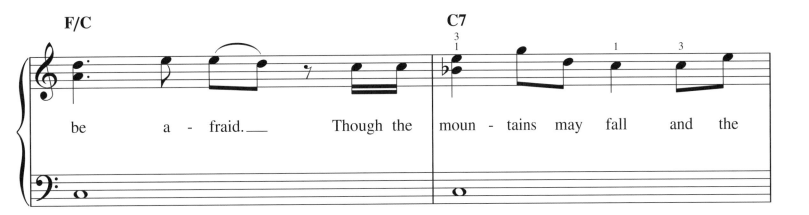

be a - fraid.___ Though the moun - tains may fall and the

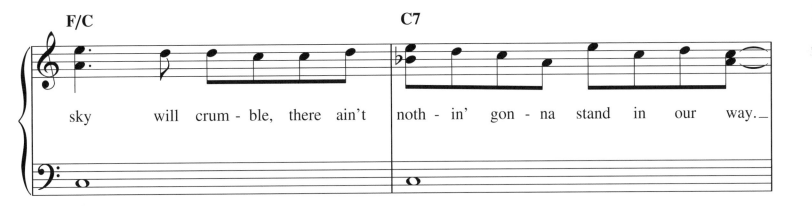

sky will crum - ble, there ain't noth - in' gon - na stand in our way.___

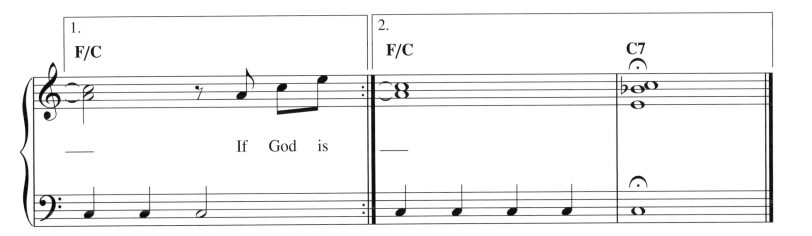

1.
F/C
___ If God is

2.
F/C ___ C7

KING OF GLORY

Words and Music by CHRIS TOMLIN
and JESSE REEVES

With praise

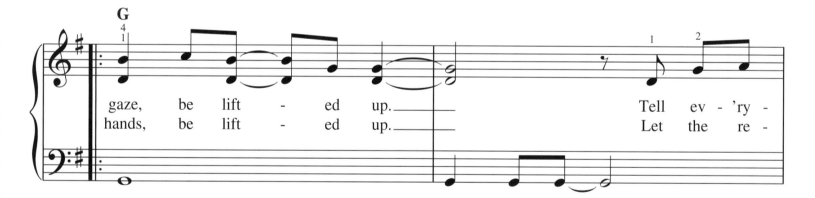

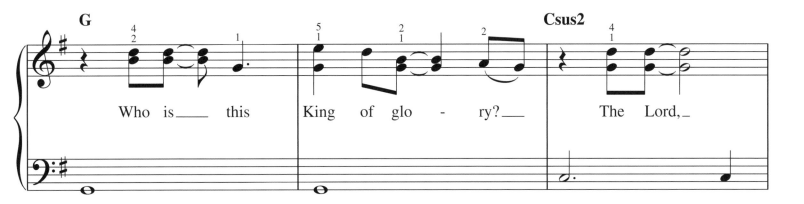

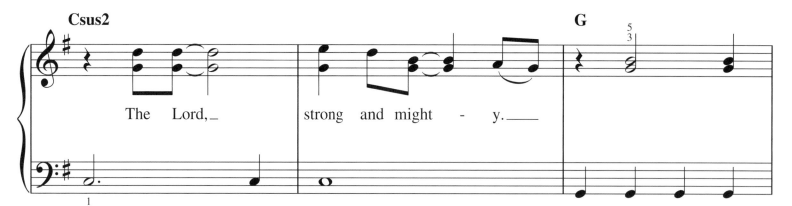

The Lord,— strong and might - y.—

Lift up your

There is one— God;— He is

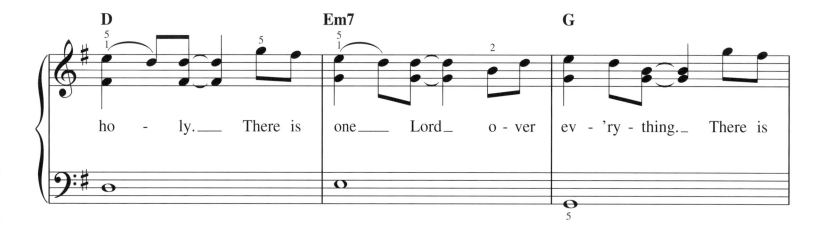

ho - ly.— There is one— Lord— o - ver ev - 'ry - thing.— There is

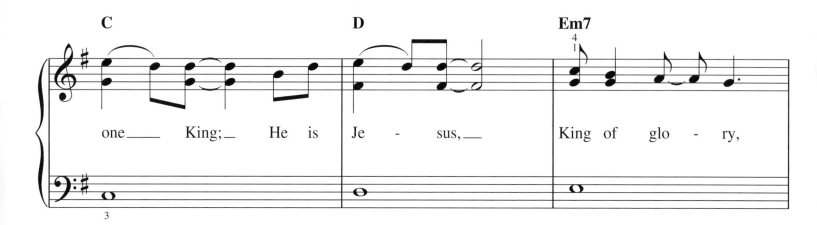

one— King; He is Je - sus,— King of glo - ry,

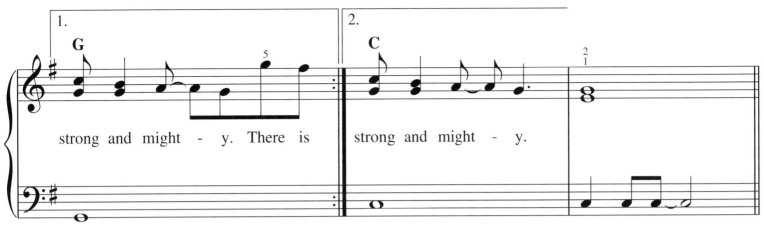

strong and might - y. There is | strong and might - y.

You are ___ the | King of glo - ry, ___ | the Lord, ___

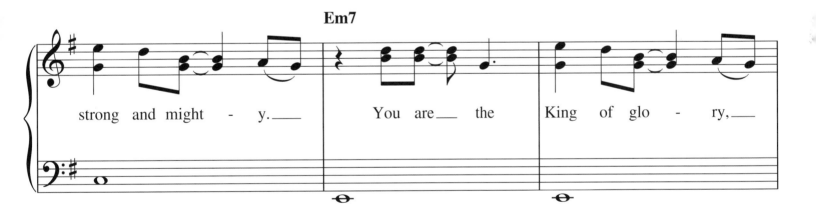

strong and might - y. ___ | You are ___ the | King of glo - ry, ___

the Lord, ___ | strong and might - y. ___

YOU DO ALL THINGS WELL

Words and Music by CHRIS TOMLIN,
JESSE REEVES and MICHAEL JOHN CLEMENT

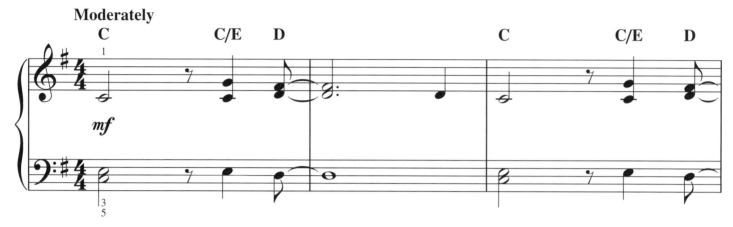

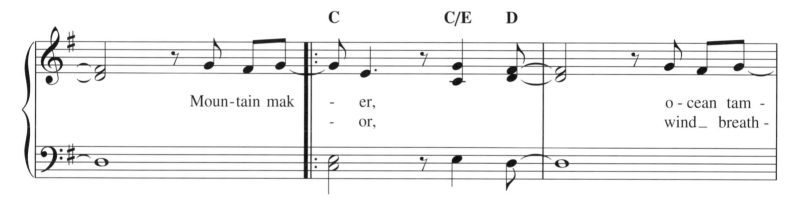

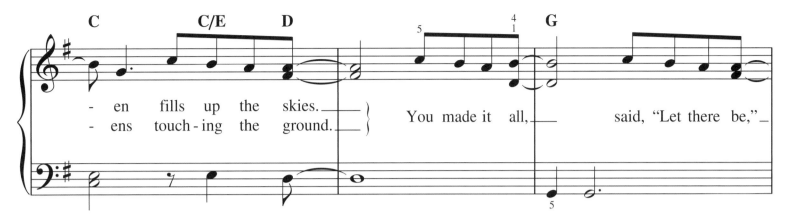

- en   fills   up   the   skies.
- ens   touch-ing   the   ground.

You made it all,   said, "Let there be,"

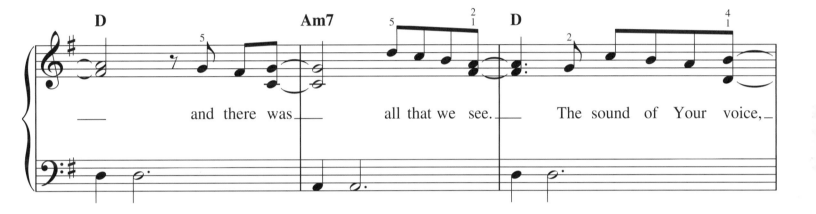

and there was   all that we see.   The sound of Your voice,

the works of Your hands,   You do all   things   well,

You do all   things   well,   You do all

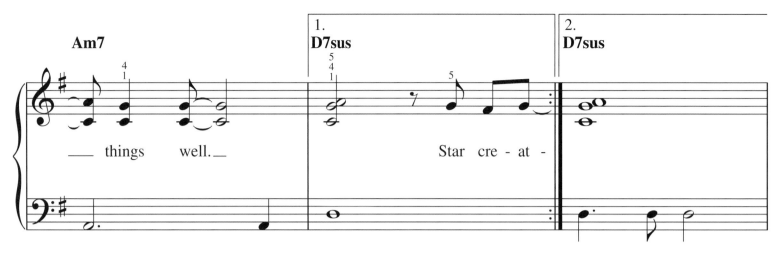

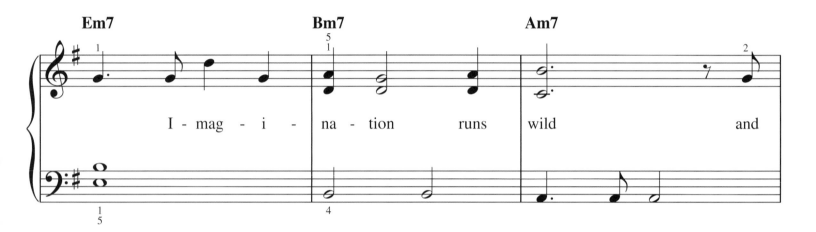

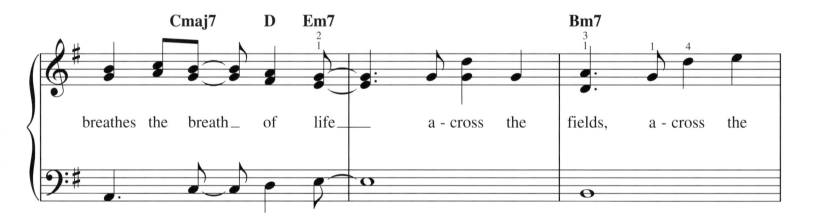

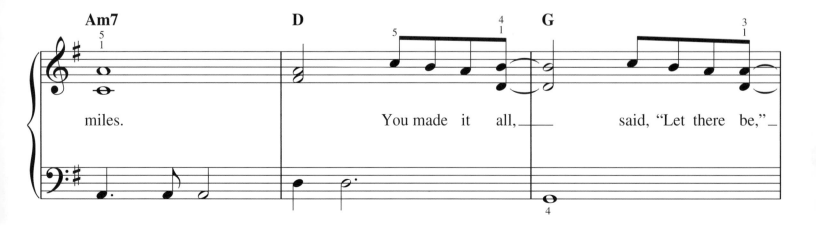

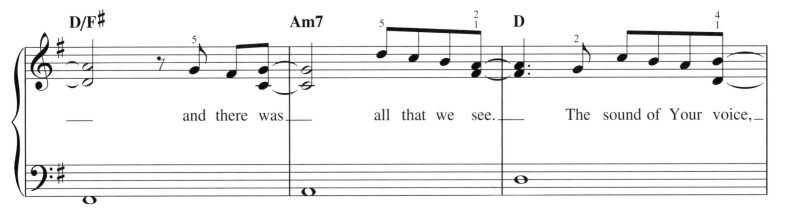

and there was____ all that we see.____ The sound of Your voice,_

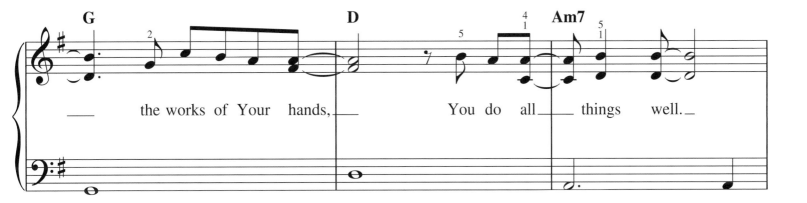

____ the works of Your hands,____ You do all____ things well._

You made it all,____ said,"Let there be,"____ and there was_

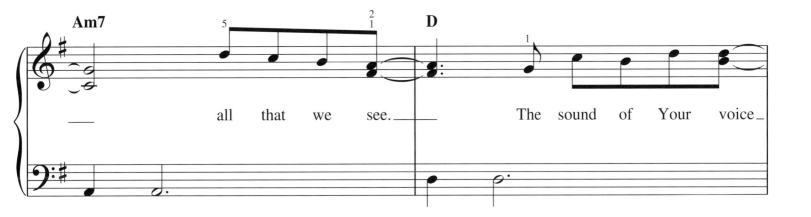

all that we see.____ The sound of Your voice_

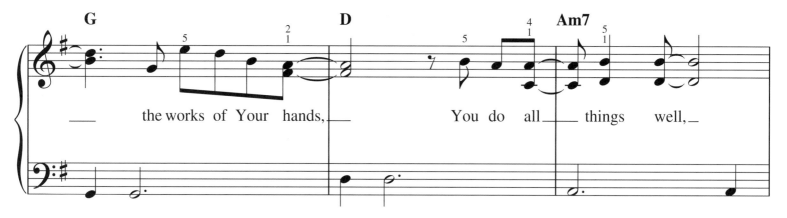

the works of Your hands,   You do all   things   well,

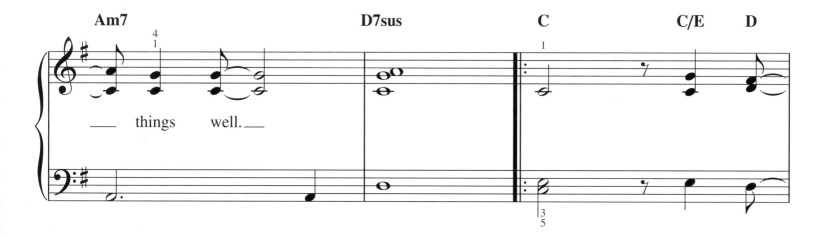

You do all   things   well,   You do all

things   well.

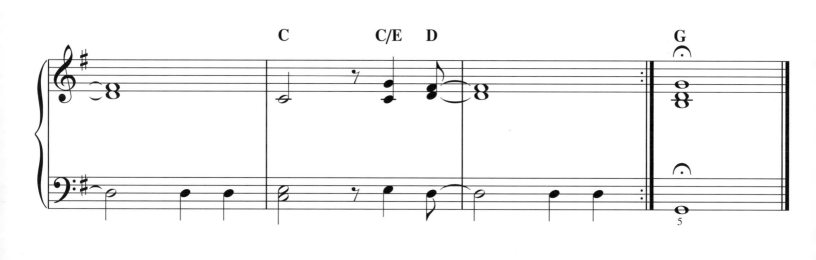